Elusive Community

Why Do We Avoid What We Were Created For?

JON ZENS

First Edition

Cover artwork: Dotty Zens
Cover design and layout: Rafael Polendo (polendo.net)

Biblical citations are taken from the *The New American Standard Bible*, modified by Jon Zens, and *The New Living Translation*, modified by Jon Zens.

ISBN 978-1-938480-58-4

This volume is printed on acid free paper and meets ANSI Z39.48 standards.

Printed in the United States of America

Published by Quoir
Orange, California

www.quoir.com

Table of Contents

Dedication

I would like to dedicate this book to Larry and Bev Lindseth. Our journeys have gone along together since the mid-1970s. Your friendship has been such a source of encouragement in the Lord.

Acknowlegments

Deep thanks to Mark Evans, Mary Ellen Robinson, Catherine Seebald and Charlene Wilder for their labor in making this a better manuscript.

Foreword

In my childhood, growing up in Kenya, the differences between the rugged individualism of the primarily American missionary station I grew up in, and the surrounding Agikuyu culture were quite dramatic.

Missionaries throughout modern history have been noted for their rugged endurance and often carrying out Lone Ranger missions—like Christian cowboys that tame the wild hearts by grit, and by insisting on a conversion of individual units. Individuals who then were quickly separated from their own cultural community.

What is striking is that all the barriers to real community described in *Elusive Community* in the Western world, with its premium on individualism, are evident and even exacerbated among missionaries on the field. The missionary stations were places of thorny discomfort as people with highly individualized callings and a plurality of beliefs developed emotional calluses, and avoided disagreement or left the mission field with hurt or shame. The fortunate missionaries were the ones who worked in remote and solitary locations.

Though I was the son of missionaries, my friendships included both children of missionaries and children of the African peoples that I grew up among.

The problems and disagreements among the Agikuyu were no less serious than the missionaries, and in many ways their issues were far more serious. They did not have the choice to pack up and go home if things got out of hand, like the missionaries did, far too often. But there was a fundamental difference in the mindset of the culture. The Agikuyu were not interested in individualism they assumed the absolute necessity of co-dependence—a version of Ubuntu philosophy, "I am because we are."

Disagreements were not handled by drawing lines but by searching for ways to erase them. There was not a time-table on resolution because resolution was not optional. Issues which would be put to a vote in the western world would be discussed, sometimes for years, because unity was more important than being right.

In essence, traditional African communities were functioning *ekklesias*. As Jon so correctly pointed out, "Paul viewed the *ekklesia* as a *problem-resolving community* . . . ." It was not in the African's cultural DNA to handle disagreements any other way. Certainly, traditional African communities benefited eternally from the knowledge of Jesus Christ and the leading of the "Spirit of Christ," but they did not need an education on community or how to function as *ekklesia*.

I do not idealize their cultures or have some notion of a Noble Savage. There are and were a host of things for which all African communities need to repent—in the classical sense of turning from their "kingdoms" to the Kingdom built without hands. This same repentance, or exchange of kingdom allegiance, is necessary for those of us grounded in Western individualism. We need to repent, not from the myriad of little foibles of being human, but from the grand kingdom we have built on individualism and turn to the Kingdom whose founder prayed that "they be as one as We are One."

Anything less than this kind of repentance and the people of God in the west will forever remain an *Elusive Community.*

> —**Skeeter Wilson,** author of *Crossing Rivers: An African Historical Fiction* and his forthcoming *Take Nothing With You: Essays on the Role of Missionaries*

Skeeter and I have been friends since 1978. His journey of nineteen years in Africa and since then in America has given him a depth that few possess.

CHAPTER ONE

We Are Heading Into Community

Some thoughts and burdens have been accumulating in my heart, and the time has come to share them. I'd like to begin by citing a profound insight Jean Vanier shared in 1988 with the Harvard Divinity School. It has to do with the transformative power of loving, accepting community—something most people, perhaps, have never experienced. Vanier served for thirty years in community with very challenged persons.

> My experience has shown that when we welcome people from this world of anguish, brokenness and depression, and when they gradually discover that they are wanted and loved as they are and that they have a place, then we witness a real transformation—I would even say "resurrection." Their tense, angry, fearful, depressed body gradually becomes relaxed, peaceful and trusting. This shows through the expression on the face and through all their flesh. As they discover a sense of belonging, that they are part of a "family," then the will to live begins to emerge (*From Brokenness to Community*, 1992, p. 15).

In *Elusive Community* I would like to give multiple perspectives from Father's heart that will encourage you to find a life of community in Christ: that the Lord would grant you the experience of love, safety and caring that Vanier spoke of. Such experience of life in Jesus with others is not plentiful—may it increase! It may be the case, as Bonnie Jaeckle pointed out, "There is limited healing in the Church because there is minimal community among God's people." For sure, it can be seen that many people are afraid of or avoid community because of how few actually pursue it. Let me unpack this observation.

CHAPTER TWO

Community in the Big Picture

When many people hear the word "community" they see the image of a hippie commune in the 1960s. But we need a revelation that community is at the heart of everything. Long ago in eternity Father, Son and Spirit were a vibrant, loving community. They determined to expand this fellowship by pursuing a Bride for the Son in the unfolding of human history—this is the eternal purpose of God in Christ.

Israel was an earthly picture of the community of God that would become a reality with the coming of the Bridegroom to earth. Jesus gathered a community around Himself during His time on earth, and when He went back to Father, He left a community of 120 men and women until the Spirit came.

In the aftermath of Jesus coming in the Spirit on the Day of Pentecost, communities of believers came to expression from house to house in Jerusalem.

After the conversion of Paul, we see the following pattern emerge as the Life of Christ comes to expression in his service to Jesus. He and other teammates would be led to a city or region and preach Christ as crucified and risen, often starting in the Jewish Synagogue. Those who believed were taught by the team about the eternal purpose of the Lord in Christ, and living by the indwelling life of Jesus. Then after varying periods of time, three weeks to over a year, Paul and his company would part from them, leaving behind a functioning assembly (*ekklesia*) with Jesus as their Leader.

In some cases the Lord allowed Paul and those with him to revisit those communities, and on a number of occasions he wrote letters to them concerning issues that were moving them away from Christ. We are not talking here about people having coffee with other believers once in awhile and calling that "church." Rather, the end result of the gospel taking root in a town would be a definable group of people who could be addressed in a letter from Paul.

In light of this early history we can see that as the gospel advanced from Jerusalem, Judea, Samaria and into Gentile regions, *the goal was for the life of Christ to be expressed in face-to-face communities of believers in each city.* The mission of Jesus was not *individualistic*, to just "get people saved." When men, women and children believed, they were baptized by the Spirit *into a body*, Christ's body on earth. We see this worked out in the Book of Acts. People believed, were baptized in water, and then started functioning together with other saints in their city: "they devoted themselves to . . . ." (Acts 2:46).

One helpful way to approach this is to consider the little town of Bethany, a few miles from Jerusalem. The hallmark of Bethany was that it was *a place where Jesus was fully welcome*. Jesus never spent a night in the "holy city" of Jerusalem—indeed, that place was the site of His death. He always went to His friends in Bethany. As far as we know, it was *the only place on earth where the red carpet was rolled out for the Lord*. For Jesus, Bethany was a special place of eating, fellowship, healing, death, resurrection, love, and learning at His feet. It must be underscored that Mary and Martha's home *was a place where Jesus' presence and will was coveted above all else*. In light of His eternal purpose in Christ, we can confidently say the Lord's heart is for Bethany-like communities to be birthed all over the earth.

CHAPTER THREE

Why Is Community So Rare?

If the New Testament reveals that vibrant community is the norm, then the question must be tendered, "Why in the history of the church has Jesus-centered community been the rare exception?"

Well, a sweeping observation of what went on in the visible church from AD 200 to AD 1600 will explain why community was virtually lost: As church leaders ascended more and more into prominence, the focus came to fall on the maintenance of the institution, and not the organic expression of Christ through the 58 one another's in the New Testament.

The union of church and state, in place since Constantine, and continued by the Protestant reformers, resulted in a conflict out of which the Anabaptist movement would arise in the 1500s. These people believed that the state should not exercise control in church matters, that state coercion in matters of conscience was wrong, and that infant baptism was not Scriptural. The Anabaptists had a strong sense of community, and practiced a simple lifestyle. The state viewed them as a threat to the status quo, and as a result they were harassed, hunted down and murdered by both Catholics and Protestants. Their writings (mostly in German) were not available in English until the 1940s, and thus Anabaptist studies have blossomed only in recent years.

CHAPTER FOUR

Community in America

The beginnings of our country that originated in England in the 1600s started with the Pilgrims (just looking for a place to worship God according to their conscience), and then the Puritans (coming with an Old Testament-rooted agenda). The Puritans saw themselves as a "New Israel," who would be crossing the Atlantic ocean (viewed as the "Red Sea"), then enter Canaan by overcoming the "heathen" (the native Indians), and finally setting up a Puritan theocracy ("a city on a hill"). There was a strong sense of community in Puritan America, but it was fueled and maintained by coercion, conformity, intimidation, the heavy-handed presence of the leaders, civil and religious, and informed by a decidedly old covenant perspective.

In the period of 1630-1880 the developing country moved westward away from New England. The pioneers faced numerous hardships as they ventured into fresh territory, much of the time not knowing what they would face in the upcoming days of their journey. Historians came to use the phrase "rugged individualism" to describe a main feature of the pioneering spirit.

"Rugged individualism" came to play a significant role in the development of frontier religion. Charles Finney was able to parlay the forces of religious individualism in a way that shaped the evangelicalism of the 19th century. Beginning in 1825 Finney preached in upstate New York. His methods, which came to be called "new measures," involved breaking people down physically and emotionally through long, loud sermons in protracted meetings, and then calling them forward to repent. The "altar call" originated around 1830.

The overwhelming focus of such meetings was to "get people saved." There was no immediate thought of having new believers function organically in a body of believers. Instead, they were expected to attend revival meetings, make a decision for Jesus and then attend one of the existing churches. No attention was given to the pattern we saw in Paul in which believing, functioning communities were left behind as he moved on to his next place to proclaim Jesus as crucified. Finney's new methods perpetuated a religious individualism that would become deeply rooted in future expressions of American evangelicalism.

At this point we need to note a bit of a paradox. While individualism was running full speed in expanding America, there were yet expressions of community popping up on two levels. First, those homesteading faced numerous obstacles, and it was common back then for neighbors to rally around the needs of others that arose. There was an underlying sense of community in those days because they knew they needed each other, given the often harsh circumstances they faced.

Secondly, especially in the 1800s, there was a surge of groups—believing and non-believing—that separated from the culture around them and formed intentional communities. The motives, aspirations, goals and beliefs of such communes varied greatly, but the glue that held them together was the hope that life would be better *together* than apart. The sad tragedy was that these would-be utopias were not founded upon and rooted in the person and work of Jesus Christ. Christ was not the heart-throb of their existence.

Some of you would profit by reading one of the following books, or one similar to them. *Utopian Communities in America, 1680—1880*, Mark Holloway; *The Search for Community*, George Melnyk; *Two Hundred Years of American Communities*, Yaacov Oved; *America's Communal Utopias*, Donald Pitzer; and *Utopias in American History*, Jyotsna Sreenivasan. Books along these lines will provide you with some nuts and bolts about how these communities began, what held them together, and the struggles they had to get along with each other.

Minus the excesses of Finney, D.L. Moody (1837-1899) carried on his legacy. Moody had the evangelistic sermon and the altar call, but his efforts got bigger as audiences packed into large tents for the meetings.

With Moody, the trend continued of an inordinate focus on "salvation," but there was no immediate integration of new believers into community body life. They may have been directed to "attend a local church," but that really had no connection to the bursting forth of Christ's life we see in Acts. "Going to church" just created people who would basically sit in pews and listen to sermons—a bunch of ears listening to a mouth.

Some seventy years later Billy Graham would come on the scene with choirs, guest celebrities, sermons, and altar calls. His added dimension was to have well-planned "crusades" in larger venues, like baseball stadiums, in order to house larger crowds. His first big crusade was in 1949 in Los Angeles.

As we have looked at a little slice of American history, we can see that *individualism* was embedded in mainstream evangelicalism, and this characteristic paralleled the rugged individualism in American culture as a whole. Perhaps you can better understand now why *community* is such a foreign concept to most, even religious people. Also, this helps us relate to why so many people would confess that they see no need for community in their lives. The American public across the board has always been ready to pull themselves up by their own bootstraps.

CHAPTER FIVE

Belonging Runs Deep

However, the Lord made us as His image, His likeness. That explains why we are wired for belonging. Father, Son and Spirit are a joyful community. Being "alone" was a problem Adam had, and Father resolved it when He brought a bride out of his side.

John Eldredge said so beautifully, "Whatever else it means to be human, we know beyond doubt that it means to be relational . . . . One of the deepest of all human longings is the longing to belong, to be a part of things, to be invited in. From this [Triune] Fellowship spring all our longings for a friend, a family, a fellowship—for someplace to belong" (*Epic*, pp. 22-24).

Even a neuropsychiatrist, Dan Seigel, pointed out, "The brain is hardwired for relationship, only a little over one-third of the brain's connections are directly or indirectly shaped by genetics. The rest are shaped by experience and interpersonal relationships."

We are *relational* beings. *We need others.* But sin has deeply and negatively impacted our connections to others. It has discouraged, twisted and perverted relationships.

Is it any wonder that people are leery of getting involved with others? For a number of reasons we run from the very thing our beings cry out for—belonging with others. Why is it that we are so gun-shy of community? One pervasive reason is that loving people often get thrown under a bus. Speaking out of much personal experience, Jack Deere noted:

> Love hurts. Anybody who has listened to a country western song knows that. But it isn't just country music is it? It's the theme of almost all music; it's the theme of art, literature and poetry. Love hurts. It hurts more than anything I've ever known. It hurt Jesus. Look what love did to Him. It led Him to the worst kind of humiliation. It led Him to a cross where He cried out, 'My God, my God, why have You forsaken me?' Love hurts, and sometimes because it hurts we find ways not to risk. We never make a conscious decision, 'I'm not going to love anymore.' But what we do is unconsciously substitute something else other than love—something that's impersonal and a lot safer than intimacy. Because intimacy opens your heart up to another person, opens your heart up to the Lord, and that's one of the most painful things you can do ("The Pain of Intimacy," cassette, 1996, Whitefish, MT).

You have listened to enough music to know that the theme of "love" among people is messy and full of paradoxes. Here are a few from among thousands of examples:

> "Only you can fill that space inside, so there's no sense pretending my heart it's not mending; just when I thought I was over you, and just when I thought I could stand on my own, oh, baby those memories come crashing

through, and I just can't go on without you." (Air Supply, "Here I am," 1981)

"[Love] heals and it hurts; she leads you to heaven's door and leaves you for dirt" (Simple Minds, "Let There Be Love," 1991)

Another deep-seated reason why people shy away from body-life is because they know how radically it would change their lifestyles. Loving, caring community involves a commitment to put others ahead of yourself—to lay your life down for your friends, just as Christ did for us. Most people just walk away from face-to-face community. When they see the dominos start to fall, the personal cost becomes too much for them to bear. That's why it's important for those pursuing community to be gripped by the Lord's eternal purpose in His Son's Bride—He desires for her to display His multi-faceted wisdom before a watching world *now*. Following the Lord's life with others is not a fad, not an experiment to try outside the institutional church—*it is to be part of the very heart of God that will culminate in the Lamb's supper with His Bride.*

So here is our serious dilemma: We are wired for rela-tionships, and the Lord has put within us a longing for belonging, but we struggle for a myriad of reasons to deeply connect with others. Barbara Streisand sang, "People who need people are the luckiest people in the world," but it looks like too many folks live life like they really don't need people in their lives. As Henri Nouwen noted with sadness, "Loneliness is one of the most universal human experiences, but our contemporary Western society has heightened the awareness of our loneliness to an unusual degree . . . . Why is it that many parties and friendly get-togethers leave us so empty and sad?" (*Reaching Out*, 1977)

CHAPTER SIX

Community in Secular Culture

As was mentioned earlier, in nineteenth century America numerous communities sprung up that separated from mainstream culture and lived close together in various configurations. Since the 1960s, a steady trickle of people have become dissatisfied with the American Dream and the stress generated by the resultant rat-race, and have opted for a simpler life with others in various forms of community.

The Foundation for Intentional Community (FIC) began in 1986, co-founded by M. Scott Peck. They have published a community directory that lists groups all over the USA and foreign countries. In general terms, Intentional Community involves people living in close proximity to each other, often on the same property. They are held together by a number of elements like charismatic personalities, causes they value, and sustainable agriculture.

Connecting housing with community has been developed by Russ Chapin in his architectural style called "Pocket Neighborhoods." His 2011 book is titled, *Pocket Neighborhoods: Creating Small Scale in a Large Scale World.*

In a December, 2019, article, Linda Sechrist gives her perspective that "the increased interest in intentional communities may hint at a possibility that the human desire for community might be nature's evolutionary nudge toward a collective leap that helps us survive a changing climate and Earth's potential sixth mass extinction" ("The Emerging Power of 'We': Awakening to the Evolution of Community," *Natural Awakenings*, December, 2019, p. 16).

In this article, Seijaku Roshi, leader of the Pine Wind Zen Community, notes that "people are searching and hungering for community, which is number one on my agenda. If we aren't talking about community, we're squandering the moment . . . . We are awakening to the fact that we're interconnected, interdependent and need community, which is the spirit and guiding light whereby people come together to fulfill a purpose, to help others fulfill their purpose and to take care of one another" (Sechrist, p. 17).

Thich Nhat Hanh suggests that "the next Buddha would likely not take form as an individual but rather as a *sangha*, a community practicing mindful living . . . . a good community is necessary for helping individuals learn how to encounter life in the present moment, resist the unwholesome ways of our time, go in the direction of peace and nourish seeds of enlightenment" (Sechrist, p. 16).

While there are some good thoughts in what Linda presents in her article, there is no *life* in such lofty ideals. The living Christ present in His body is nowhere in her picture.

CHAPTER SEVEN

What About Christ-driven Community?

From pictures we find in the New Testament there are certain patterns of Spirit-led life together. The ethos of new covenant community life is unveiled in Acts 2—

"They were continually devoting themselves to the apostles' teaching and to fellowship, to the breaking of bread and to prayer. Everyone kept feeling a sense of awe; and many wonders and signs were taking place through the apostles. And all those who had believed were together and had all things in common; and they began selling their property and possessions and were sharing them with all, as anyone might have need. Day by day continuing with one mind in the temple, and breaking bread from house to house, they were taking their meals together with gladness and sincerity of heart, praising God and having favor with all the people. And the Lord was adding to their number day by day those who were being saved." (NASB)

Perhaps *The Diary of Anne Frank* provides one of the best (but limited) windows into the realities of the community life we are talking about. In June, 1942, eight Jewish people were thrust into hiding in an upstairs attic in Holland during Hitler's reign.

For our purposes here, three observations are worthy of pointed attention. One, eight diverse people found themselves in one living space together. Two, if they wanted to stay alive, they could not leave their attic living quarters. Three, they could not run away from their tiny space—they had no choice but to forge out the details of life together for over two years.

The events in Anne's *Diary* highlight some key realities believing communities should ponder. What these eight people were forced to do in order to survive, shouldn't we do with our brothers and sisters in Christ freely from our hearts?

- They were close to each other—"in your face," in the best sense.

- They cared for and shared with one another.

- They did not run away, but stayed to participate in the joys, sorrows, the ups and downs of being a community.

- With their diverse personalities and quirks, they learned to work through the tough issues that arose in their life together.

You might be saying, "This is pretty heavy duty interpersonal stuff; will His life in us lead to such face-to-face body-life?" Well, let's think about the revelation of community in the words of Jesus and Paul for a while.

In Matthew 18 Jesus spelled out the basics of conflict resolution in His body, the *ekklesia*. If one sins against another, they are to meet one-on-one. If reconciliation is not effected, then several others are brought along to help in the resolution of the problem. Then Jesus said, "if he/she refuses to listen to them, tell it to the *ekklesia*; and if he/she refuses to listen to the *ekklesia*, treat him/her as you would a pagan or a tax collector."

The process Jesus shared reveals some crucial assumptions about the community He envisioned.

- It assumes the saints *knew each other.* You simply could not carry out this way of problem resolution *without the group being in relational life together.*

- It assumes that in the body *the life of the Lord brought them to a level of commitment by which they would stick around to work through issues, and not run away.* It took a pretty high level of commitment to handle the problems present in Corinth.

- It assumes there was a community that shared Christ's life together. They loved one another and functioned together. As a group they could receive words from Jesus (as in His evaluations of the seven *ekklesias* in Revelation), or from an itinerant person like Paul.

- They saw themselves as having Christ's blessing to bind and loose—to use the Keys
  of the Kingdom and pursue His mind
  in everything they faced together.

Also consider one of Paul's letters to Corinthian believers. Paul saw a lot of grace and gifts in the Corinthian saints,
but they also had a boatload of problems. There was a case
of immorality that they had not addressed. There were disputes between some of the brethren and they were taking
each other before unbelieving judges. In the first case, Paul
told them to come together as a body and take care of the
matter in a way that echoes Matthew 18. In the second
case, he told them to arbitrate disputes within the body by
finding persons of wisdom to help.

Paul viewed the *ekklesia* as a *problem-resolving community* led by the Spirit of Christ. He reasoned from the
greater to the lesser: "Don't you know that the saints will
judge the world? And if the world is judged by you, are you
unworthy to judge small issues? Don't you know we will
judge angels? How much more matters in this life!"

In order for the directives Paul gave to be carried out,
a spiritual component had to be present and functioning:
commitment. Think about it. How could you get a group of
people to gather and make the decision to hand an unre-
pentant person over to the evil one? How could you ask an
assembly to stop bringing disputes to secular courts and
work the problematic issues out among themselves? There
is no way Paul's words to the Corinthians would make any

sense at all without his conviction that there was among them a *commitment to Jesus to carry out His will in their relationships with other brothers and sisters.*

I hope you can see from what has been presented so far that "going to church" is not the same as being part of a gospel community fueled by the life of Christ. A sister shared her experience with me recently. "People can attend services to hear a teaching but never experience any community or even know people in the church. I remember introducing myself to a person sitting next to me at a local, larger church and she said she had been coming for three years but didn't know anyone."

When have you seen or heard of any churches in your town, or in distant localities, ever practicing *as a body* what Paul assumed the Corinthians could do? How can they? The commitment level to one another is generally very low. As M. Scott Peck astutely observed, what people usually see are "churches that lack community and the spirit of community . . . churches where the members don't seem to take the rule of Christ seriously" (*The Different Drum*, p. 303).

When churches in America have problems of all sorts, the members tend to *run away from the conflict.* When Paul gave words of correction and restoration to the *ekklesias*, he assumed the believers *would stay and pursue the Lord together with a view toward working matters out.*

CHAPTER EIGHT

How Can Ekklesia be a Relational Reality?

You may be scratching your head, saying, "How can we be a loving community that loves Jesus so much that we can stick it out together and not run away?" The simple answer is: *We cannot do community in and of ourselves; we can only love one another by His life in us—"I am the vine, you are the branches, and you can do nothing without Me."*

Why was Paul confident that the believing communities he left behind were capable of sustaining their life together without his presence? There is only one answer: *He knew that Christ was in them by the Spirit, and that His life would come to expression through the ekklesia.*

It is about *Life*—Christ's life. His life continues on earth through His body, the *ekklesia*. Jesus came on the Day of Pentecost in the Spirit to inaugurate a *new humanity*, the *ekklesia*, a *new creation*, a *Third Race*, and a *new species*. Jesus' words, "I will come to you," are the foundation for all the explosive spiritual activity after Pentecost. The saints were driven by the *Life of Jesus in them*. They had no Bibles, no buildings, no liturgies, no charismatic leaders, no budgets, and no programs. The Jesus movement sprang from *His life—rivers of living water flowing from His saints.*

Frank Viola gets to the heart of what is vital in a community of Jesus' people:

> When a group of believers makes Jesus Christ central, He is reflected in their conversations, their sharing, their ministry, their meetings, their songs—and their very lives . . . . To put it candidly, you will never have an authentic experience of the body of Christ unless your foundation is blindly and singularly Jesus Christ. Authentic church life is born when a group of people are intoxicated with a glorious unveiling of their Lord . . . . the church is a local group of people who have been immersed and saturated with a magnificent vision of Jesus Christ and who are discovering how to take Him as their All together and bring Him to the world (*From Eternity to Here*).

You can't "start" a Jesus community. Kingdom community must be "birthed." Over the past years, I've seen comments like this one on Facebook: "Anyone here live near --------? I will be starting an Organic church in my coffee shop at the end of January. Would love to have you join in"(12/21/19). Well-meaning people have started a lot of groups, but very few of them are ever *birthed* by the Lord's Spirit.

No one can give you a "how-to" regarding community. Organic *ekklesia* can have no formula. "Here are 12 steps. Do these and you'll have community." In the New Testament, communities were birthed when Paul came into a locale and proclaimed Christ as crucified, and some believed in Jesus. For varying periods of time Paul opened up God's eternal purpose in His Son, showed aspects of living in the New Humanity, and then left a community of believers behind as the Lord moved him on to the next destination.

CHAPTER NINE

Who Do You Want Walking With You in the Cool of the Day?

We tend to jump prematurely to the form we think will best facilitate the fruition of the *ekklesia* we envision. This is a huge mistake. Wouldn't it be best to first focus on what the Lord Jesus would desire *in us*? What kind of living stones contribute to the building up of Jesus' house? There are many Spirit-fruits that could be considered, but these are the seven that came to my heart.

- Community is fostered by those who are constrained by the love of Christ.

- Community is calmed by those whose demeanor is marked by humility.

- Community is facilitated by those who are slow to speak and quick to hear.

- Community is strengthened by those who have a teachable spirit.

- Community is reinforced by those who have patience with others.

- Community is encouraged by those who are in step with "submit to one another out of reverence for Christ."

- Community is energized by those with caring hearts.

None of us are perfect in these qualities, and we all have struggles in different areas. But, hopefully, we would ask the Lord to bring these seven qualities more and more visibly into our daily lives. If a community is defective in many of these attributes, you can easily see how it would be very hard for them to survive.

> For where jealousy and selfish ambition exist, there will be disorder and every evil practice. But the wisdom from above is first of all pure, then peaceable, gentle, accommodating, full of mercy and good fruit, impartial, and sincere (James 3:17).

But here's where it gets tricky. Community cannot be about people whose ducks seem to be in a row. People may come into the group who are deeply wounded, and bring with them all kinds of heavy baggage. The image of a hospital could rightly be connected to a loving community.

> Community groups should be therapeutic, inasmuch as they assist members to grow to the fullness of their life in Christ. People need to see a group of persons, motivated

by the gospel and their love of God, who live in such a way that loneliness and alienation are dispelled (Hammett & Sofield, ST, 1996).

Groups, of course, will vary in their ability to care for others. Some persons will need professional help of various kinds. But we must not underestimate how the Lord can use a caring community in all of our lives. As Henri Nouwen pointed out, "We are all healers who can reach out to offer health, and we are all patients in constant need of help . . . . We can do much more for each other than we often are aware of . . . . A general atmosphere of careful attention by all the members of the Christian community can sometimes heal wounds before special care is demanded" (*Reaching Out*, 1975, pp. 93, 94, 97).

J. Jeffrey Means clinical findings led him to conclude that there were three dilemmas facing the church regarding ministry to those set back by trauma. His perspectives, however, apply to the general life of Christ in the assembly.

> The dilemmas are: (1) how to make better and more effective use of the shared life experiences of its members within the worship and life of the church, (2) how to encourage people to bring into the worship and life of the church those aspects of themselves and their life experience they are most ashamed of and split-off from, and (3) how to talk about sin in a way that takes it seriously but does not shame us or lead us to view ourselves and others dichotomously as "all good" or "all bad" . . . . [The future of the church is tied into] the extent to which the church will be a place that offers care and support to those who have been hurt by violence or abuse, and the extent to

which the church will offer an environment of healing for those elements within people that set them up to interact with others in hurtful ways (J. Jeffrey Means, *Trauma & Evil: Healing the Wounded Soul*, Fortress Press, 2000, pp. 178-182).

The early *ekklesia* was made up of a number of very diverse people groups—Jews, Greeks, circumcised, uncircumcised, male, female, slaves, free, barbarian and Scythian. They were all part of the New Humanity Jesus created through His cross. I do not think we begin to comprehend how hard it would be, humanly speaking, for such believers to get along and eat together in the communities where they lived. Only the love of Christ flowing through them could hold them together! No wonder Paul would say to the Colossians, "So, as those who have been chosen of God, holy and beloved, put on a heart of compassion, kindness, humility, gentleness and patience."

CHAPTER TEN

Do We Want to Build Up the Body?

Chuck Swindoll spoke about "grace killers" in his book, *The Grace Awakening*. Unfortunately, there can be behaviors in us that are potential community killers. There are many such ways of acting, but I would like to deal with the ones I've seen manifested the most over the years. If the Spirit touches us about certain issues in our life that could hinder Christ's flow in the body, would we ask the Lord to deal with them?

Let's imagine ourselves in a living-room group. What words and actions could be expressed that might sap the life out of a gathering? Here are some:

- Persons constantly bring up their personal agendas and preferences. They wear their convictions and scruples on their sleeves.

- Persons come across to others as if they have to be right. They won't let go of their viewpoint.

- Persons interrupt others before they can finish their thoughts. They are not really listening to others, but wanting to insert their ideas before others can complete their sentences.

- Persons intimidate others by the way they forcefully speak, and by the body language they display. This causes others to shut down and clam up.

- Persons present themselves as know-it-alls. They give the impression that there is little they need to learn.

- Persons whose comments are laced with performance-based imperatives—"we've got to do this, we've got to do that," and "God won't love us if we do this or that."

- Persons who talk too much. They often go on and on when they don't have anything of substance to offer.

- Persons who talk too little. For various reasons, such people are afraid to share, and may think they have nothing to offer. Such need to be encouraged that they indeed have a unique and important portion of Christ to share.

- Persons who are leader wannabes think that they should run the meeting, pick the songs, do a teaching, and be the go-to source for the direction of the body.

- Persons who are judgmental in their spirits, and thereby want to portray themselves as better than others.

- Persons who are controlling and dominating must
  have everything done according to their wishes,
  and their viewpoints are usually fixed in concrete.

In a relationally-based community, issues like these, and
many more, can be dealt with as the brothers and sisters
sharpen one another through body life. It does not mean
that all will be worked out harmoniously, but it does mean
people will have opportunities for growth, and that community killers can be addressed. Vibrant body-life during
the week goes a long way to help smooth the rough edges
in the group.

CHAPTER ELEVEN

It's Always Something

There are no utopias in Christ-centered community. "To wait for moments or places where no pain exists, no separation is felt and where all human restlessness has turned into inner peace is waiting for a dream-world" (Nouwen, *Reaching Out*). Besides the challenges of getting along with each other, there are issues that come up time and again that can seriously distract the group. When such matters arise, the brothers and sisters must seek the Lord's mind in resolving conflicts. Remember, there are a hundred doctrinal and practical concerns that could be listed, but these are the ones that have come up repetitively in my experience.

- Geography is a continual issue in America. It is hard for body-life to flourish when people are spread out all over town. Groups have to ask the Lord how they can maximize their fellowship during the week in an organic way.

- In many groups, the husband and wife are not on the same page regarding *ekklesia*. One might be quite happy with a traditional church setting, while the other sees the Bride quite differently. The couple should work together to be one-minded, but the chemistry and circumstances of each marriage are such that the outcome cannot be predicted.

- "What to do with the children?" has generated much discussion in groups. This issue gives the brethren an opportunity to seek the Lord for resolution to a sensitive matter.

- Often there will be a family that comes out of a church tradition in which the sisters were instructed to be silent. This is a touchy concern, and it can generate heat instead of light. If people believe it is wrong for women to participate, it will be very difficult for a group to function peacefully with both sides present in the living room.

- Food was a huge problem in the early church. Think about believers from Jewish and Gentile backgrounds having a meal together. The Gentiles would pretty much eat anything, but the Jews had a number of issues with "unclean" foods. In our day, there is the possibility of rifts occurring over such things as organic versus GMO foods. I know of a group that years ago split because some brethren insisted that organic cane sugar be used instead of processed white sugar. Paul's perspective is clear: "Nothing is unclean of itself . . . . The kingdom of

> God is not about eating and drinking, but righteousness, and peace and joy in the Holy Spirit."

- Unfortunately, not a few are uptight about the "correct" version of the Bible. By advocating that only one version is valid—the King James for example—many problems are created, and more division is spawned among God's people. If a person wishes to read the KJV, that is fine, but there are a number of good Bible translations, and none of them are perfect.

- Many groups have suffered distraction and resultant quarreling by some who push an Israel-centered view of history. It was around 1830 when J.N. Darby began to propagate his two-purposes theory, that God has an earthly purpose for Israel and a heavenly one for the church. The ripples from this notion are still with us today, as is evidenced in much of the Bible-teaching heard on the radio, television and in pulpits and Bible colleges. However, the Lord only has one eternal purpose in His Son. The Psalmist said, "Kiss the Son," not Israel (Psalm 2:12).

We have a distinct propensity to move away from Jesus to other concerns and diversions. That is why a community must be vigilant in eating and drinking of Christ alone in their life together.

CHAPTER TWELVE

A Good Dose of Reality

Sometimes when people get a glimpse of the Lord's eternal purpose in the Son, they become obsessed with finding Mecca, the perfect spot, the pristine *ekklesia*. Henri Nouwen has isolated this phenomenon superbly:

> It is this fear that makes us so intolerant toward our own loneliness and makes us grab prematurely for what seem to be 'final solutions' . . . . It is sad to see how sometimes people suffering from loneliness, often deepened by the lack of affection in their intimate family circle, search for a final solution for their pains and look at a new friend, a new lover or a new community with Messianic expectations . . . . their hearts keep saying, 'Maybe this time I have found what I have knowingly or unknowingly been searching for' (*Reaching Out*, 1977).

We must recall, however, Paul's designation of this present age as *firstfruits*. In this life we will never get the whole enchilada. There are three *groans* the Lord has given to remind us that we look for a resurrection *harvest* in the future—our inner groan for the age to come, the creation's groan for liberation from the curse, and the Spirit's intercession for us with groanings too deep for words (Romans 8).

The *ekklesia* is now an icon of the coming new heaven and new earth, but it is still *partial*. This is why we are saved in hope of the resurrection into the wedding supper of the Lamb where there will be no more curse and no more tears.

CHAPTER THIRTEEN

"The Spirit and the Bride Say, 'Come'"

Why is there so little community since we were created for belonging? There are a number of historical and cultural factors that account for this, but I believe there is one key, overwhelming reason for the paucity of face-to-face communities: *we have separated what God's eternal purpose has joined together—life in His Son is part and parcel of life in His body, His Bride and His ekklesia.* The New Exodus in Jesus' cross both delivers us from sin and *brings us into His body, the New Humanity.*

Paul expressed it like this: "for by one Spirit we were all baptized into one body—Jews or Greeks, slaves or free— and all were made to drink of one Spirit." When we come to Christ for the forgiveness of sins, we also come into His one body.

"I am born again into a family" (Jonathan and Melissa Hesler, "No Longer Slaves," Bethel Music)

The problem is very few people have any consciousness of being in a family after they come to Christ for salvation. This should alert us to the fact that in "evangelism," we are not just getting people to say a prayer," we are inviting them into a new life—a life of following Christ and a life of functioning in His body (which cannot be equated with "going to church"). We are appealing to them to enter into *life* in Jesus and with His brothers and sisters.

Our individualistic approach to the believer's life should be replaced by the body dimension found in Paul's writings. Paul envisioned Christ in us being lived out in a community of His people. Underscore his pattern: in Romans 1-11 he opened up gospel issues, then in 12-16 he fleshed out life in the body; in Ephesians 1-3 he unfolded the Lord's eternal purpose in Christ, then in 4-6 he shared about functioning in the body; in Colossians 1-2 he unveiled the glorious Christ, then in 3-4 he spoke about the body working together. First Paul gives the indicative (you have been made alive with Christ), then he issues the imperative (now live in line with who you are).

Think specifically about Ephesians 4:1-7. After opening up the mystery of God in Christ in chapters 1-3, then in chapter 4 he implores them to live in a way that is in line with their new life. In verses 2-3 we see that this new way of living takes place in community life, "with all lowliness and meekness, with patience, forbearing one another in love, eager to maintain the unity of the Spirit in the bond of peace." Paul's words have no meaning without the assumption that he is speaking to a group of believers in committed relationships to one another where they live.

Notice that Paul does not begin or even mention individual activities like "pray, read your Bible, attend a

Bible study and go to a Bible-believing church." Instead, he begins with traits that are embedded in local ongoing relationships. When look at the back of someone's head weekly, how does being forbearing with that person have any meaning? What sense can be made of forbearing if it is applied to a person one sees a handful of times a year? The New Testament epistles reveal that everywhere the gospel went, believing communities were left behind. "We ourselves boast of you in the *ekklesias* of God for your steadfastness" (2 Thessalonians 1:4).

CHAPTER FOURTEEN

"Let Us Consider One Another"

There are 58 one anothers in the New Testament, including love one another, be longsuffering with one another, support one another and exhort one another. Think of the particular "one anothers" found in Hebrews 10:24-25, "let us consider how to stir up one another to love and good works, not abandoning our gathering together, like some are doing, but encouraging [one another], and all the more as you see the day drawing near." The verb "consider" involves giving pointed mental attention to something, in this case believers one assembles with. Of course, you can "consider" people who are far away, but the writer here has in view believers you know and are relationally involved with. To "consider" others—what their needs are, how you can serve them—again highlights the reality that the early *ekklesia* was a closely-knit community, learning to work out His life in them with others.

CHAPTER FIFTEEN

God's Kingdom is Relational

I'm guessing that many of you are resonating with what I have presented concerning the Lord's heart for community, but you are frustrated, perhaps weary, because you find your family in a spiritual wilderness. I have two suggestions.

First, *pray*. Pray that Jesus would build His *ekklesia* where you are. Pray that He would bring people across your path who are hungry, asking questions. Pray that He would deepen relationships with those you already know. Pray that Christ's kingdom will come, which means that relationships will flourish. We know we cannot wave a wand and make community happen. We dare not try to manufacture relationships. But we can pray to the master *ekklesia*-Builder and ask Him to manifest Himself in Bethany-like communities where we live and all over the earth. If we pray in line with His heart—His eternal purpose in the Son—we know He will not give us a stone or a scorpion. It probably won't happen overnight, but Jesus' kingdom will come, and He has already come to dwell in us!

Second, consider how you can use *hospitality* to get to know people around you, and develop relationships.

These days opening your home in many places is not so easy. Many people just want to be left alone and some are very skeptical of going into a home for games or a meal. The individualism in our culture is very deep. I suggest three reading recommendations to encourage you in your expression of hospitality.

- Christine Pohl, *Making Room: Recovering Hospitality as a Christian Tradition*

- Barry Jones, "The Dinner Table as a Place of Connection, Brokenness and Blessing," (DTS *Voice*) https://voice.dts.edu/ article/a-place-at-the-table-jones-barry/

- Miriam Weinstein, *The Surprising Power of Family Meals*, 2006.

CHAPTER SIXTEEN

Will We Pursue What We Were Created For?

Obviously, I cannot cover every nook and cranny related to the revelation of *ekklesia*-community in the New Testament and how it is rooted in the Lord's eternal purpose to secure a Bride for His Son. But I trust that the various perspectives that have been provided will stir you up to seek Jesus about connecting His life in you with His life in others.

These are the points that must be underscored and that will hopefully grip our innermost parts: *The Lord has designed for face-to-face communities to appear wherever the gospel takes root on the earth; He desires for these ekklesias to continue and display the ministry of Christ on earth; thus, community is not just optional icing on the cake—it is part of the cake itself.* Here is how Paul put it, in part:

> For he has made known to us in all wisdom and insight the mystery of his will, according to his purpose which he set forth in Christ . . . . In him, according to the purpose of him who accomplishes all things according to the counsel of his will . . . . to make all people see what is the plan of the mystery hidden for ages in God who created

all things; that through the *ekklesia* the manifold wisdom of God might now be made known to the principalities and powers in heavenly places. This was according to the eternal purpose which he has realized in Christ Jesus our Lord (Ephesians 1:9, 11; 3:9-11).

Community and its implications are not popular options, but they comprise the Lord's heart. This is the question we must face, *is the Lord's passion our passion too?*

The home, the intimate place, the place of true belonging, is, therefore, not a place made by human hands. It is fashioned for us by God, who came to pitch his tent among us, invite us to his place, and prepare a room for us in his own home (Henri Nouwen, *You Are the Beloved*, p. 38).

"Human beings will go to any lengths necessary to find and connect with each other. It doesn't matter the technology." (Eric Whitacre, "A Virtual Choir 2,000 Voices Strong," Youtube)

CHAPTER SEVENTEEN

Afterword, April, 2020

I'm now in Tucson, Arizona, finishing up the manuscript of *Elusive Community* for publication. In light of the many concerns surrounding the intrusion of the CoronaV, it is appropriate to reflect on how this disease has so far affected what is called "church" in light of some prophetic remarks I made in 1981.

What are three key pillars that church leaders connect with practicing church in America? *Building to meet in; pastor to give sermon; a way to collect tithes.* All three of these have been deeply challenged by the in-your-face enormity of the CoronaV problem. The buildings cannot be used for services. The pastor's sermon is now found on-line. Tithing has to be done electronically or by mail. If this goes on long enough, will church leaders be sweating about how their salaries will be met, and how building costs will be maintained?

Do you think people will realize that the essential components of "church" that have been practiced for hundreds of years need to be revisited and evaluated? Will they have a

revelation that the body of Christ is about relationships—
the 58 one anothers in the New Testament?

In 1981 I closed my article, "Building Up the Body:
One Man or One Another?" with these words:

> Some might feel that churches are not "ready" for the
> truths that have been discussed in this article. But why
> should *truth* be postponed? Were churches "ready" to
> practice the responsibilities of priesthood a hundred years
> ago? Fifty? Twenty? If years of tradition are wrong, just
> when will we be "ready" to edify one another as we should?
> If something important is missing in our churches, then
> the time has come for us to implement what Christ has
> revealed. The implications of a functioning priesthood
> probably seem "radical" only because we are used to pat-
> terns of tradition which have no foundation in Scripture.

> We must ask ourselves if our churches are being prepared
> for future suffering. *Our current "freedoms" with reference
> to assembling together may be disrupted some day by govern-
> mental upheaval.* Are the saints being prepared *now* to
> care and sacrifice for one another? What if all evangelical
> pastors were arrested? Would the churches be in a position
> to continue functioning? *The possibility of an underground
> church in the future (which is a reality in many places) should
> cause us to reflect upon our preparedness for such a situation.*
> Learning to care and minister to one another now is an
> essential.

> The church traditions built around one "office" and
> the personality that occupies the pulpit is a monumen-
> tal aberration. This model portrays the idea that the body
> of Christ depends on *one part*. Unless and until we cast
> out this demon-like paradigm once and for all, we will

just continue to suppress the full expression of Christ which comes only through the *many parts*.

It has been 40 years since 1981. Now it is 2020. Churches have not changed, just different Band-Aids cover over the problems. There is a way to reality and authenticity in Christ: simplicity. Eugene Peterson in *The Pastor: A Memoir* (HarperOne, 2011) acknowledges that "the first three centuries of Christian churches were cave churches—unobtrusive house churches and catacombs" (p. 170).

It seems that these facts from history are usually glossed over as if they stand as an irrelevant footnote for us. I would like to suggest that a pattern of Christ-centered simplicity unfolds in the New Testament. Jesus desires for himself to be expressed through his body in this age (Eph. 3:10). The *ekklesias* of the first century were relational face-to-face communities. Eugene notes that "all the great realities that we can't touch or see take form on ground that we *can* touch and see" (p. 12). I agree. Which means that, to a watching world, the invisible heavenly realities on earth can only be seen *in the properly functioning body of Christ*—where *all* parts express Christ, not just a select few paid staff.

A MARGINAL MINORITY

A most profound insight comes from Peterson in his persuasion that *smallness,* not largeness, will be most effective in forwarding Christ's kingdom.

> [I came to] a developing conviction that the most effective strategy for change, for revolution—at least on the large scale that the Kingdom of God involves—comes from a minority working from the margins . . . . That a minority people working from the margins has the best chance of being a community capable of penetrating the non-community, the mob, the depersonalized, function-defined crowd that is the sociological norm of America (p. 16).

It is my heart-felt conviction that this *marginal minority* will penetrate our alienated, wounded, impersonal culture best with people functioning outside of the institutional church. The traditional pastor-centered form is just not going to cut it—from a biblical or pragmatic perspective. Eugene asked his pastor friend, after he expressed frustration about being pulled away from vital relationships "because I have to run this damn church"—*Why did he find the diner a more hospitable venue for being a pastor than the church?*

What catastrophe must come for us to awaken to the fact that pastor-centered churches have never equipped people to relationally pursue the 58 one anothers in the New Testament? What are we going to do when "the pastor" and the Tithe are gone? Frederick Buechner noted that support groups like AA are "far closer to what Christ meant his Church to be," and "they make you wonder if the best thing that could happen to many a church might not be to have its building burn down and to lose all its money. Then all that the people would have left is Christ and each other."

Again, as I prophesied in 1981: "*Our current 'freedoms' with reference to assembling together may be disrupted some day by governmental upheaval.* . . . the possibility of an underground church in the future (which is a *reality* in many places) should cause us to reflect upon our preparedness for such a situation. Learning to care and serve one another now is an essential."

—JZ, April 2, 2020

CHAPTER EIGHTEEN

America, Land of Lost Community

PAUL L. WACHTEL

[This material appeared in *Searching Together*, Vol. 38:3-4, 2012. There can be little doubt that an aggressive individualism reigns in America. The "community sense" that used to be stronger here is virtually lost in the 21ˢᵗ century. But, does what is calling itself "church" even foster and cultivate living community, or does it contribute to the individualistic status quo? In the midst of a culture that is falling apart, the Body of Christ is to be an organic setting where the multi-faceted wisdom of God is manifested in and through the saints—a new humanity, a new community which is radically counter-cultural—a setting where the only medium of exchange is love—a family community where Christ's shared life is lived out among the brothers and sisters as the visible Life expression of Christ in and to a needy world. Wachtel mentions "the widespread yearning for greater closeness to others." It is clear that people will not find this in the culture at large. Many are looking for love in all the wrong places. Will they find that "greater closeness to others" in Christ's *ekklesia*? —JZ]

"SOCIAL NEUROSIS"

Something about our commitment to [economic] growth seems akin to the phenomena observed in individual neuroses. For me the heart of the notion of neurosis is the occurrence of vicious cycles in people's behavior in which their sense of security is undermined by the very efforts they make to bolster it. In what follows I shall examine how our quest for economic growth has been both a cause of drastic changes in the way we live, and a cornerstone of our efforts to deal with the anxiety generated by those very changes . . . .

TIGHTLY KNIT COMMUNITY GONE

In explicating further, I wish to begin not with economic growth per se but with the sense of community and its decline. For most of human history people lived in tightly knit communities in which each individual had a specified place, and in which there was a strong sense of shared fate. The sense of belonging, of being part of something larger than oneself, was an important source of comfort. In the face of the dangers and the terrifying mysteries that the lonely individual encountered, this sense of connectedness—along with one's religious faith, which often could hardly be separated from one's membership in the community—was for most people the main way of achieving some sense of security and the courage to go on.

Over the past few hundred years, for a number of reasons, the sense of rootedness and belonging has been declining. In its place has appeared a more highly differentiated sense of individuality, implying both greater opportunity and greater separateness . . . .

This does not mean, of course, that *some* sense of community, and *some* secure ties to others do not remain. We could not survive without such ties . . . . While there is much truth in the common claim that individualism arose in the Renaissance, that claim must be understood as referring to individualism as a vector that began to challenge that of rootedness as the central force in society, not as a new phenomenon altogether.

The facts of our separate bodies, our separate pain, our separate deaths, as well as the differences in temperament and personality . . . preclude the possibility of a complete absence of individual identity and a sense of separateness . . . . This understood, it may be stated strongly that we have witnessed a striking increase in the sense of separate, differentiated identity and a corresponding sharp decline in the sense of community and belonging.

SOCIAL MOBILITY

The sense of belonging and shared fate has been further eroded by the social and geographic mobility that are far more characteristic of our society than of previous ones . . . . One out of five of us moves each year. Today our place in the social order is less clearly demarcated and less securely held. We have no reserved seats. We must *win* our place.

We have friends, of course, but they are friends who have *chosen* us . . . . Jeremy Seabrook refers to the "strangers who live where neighborhoods once were" . . . .

Our enormously greater capacity to predict and control events, to alleviate pain and hunger, to provide leisure and abundance *should* have made us happier. Life now shouldn't be just different, it should be better, much better . . . . That, I think, is not the case . . . .

'SECURITY' IN POSSESSIONS

Our present stress of growth and productivity is, I believe, intimately related to the decline in rootedness. Faced with loneliness and vulnerability that come with deprivation of a securely encompassing community, we have sought to quell the vulnerability through our possessions . . . . But the comfort we achieve tends to be short-lived.

In all eras people must find means to reassure themselves in the face of their finiteness and mortality. We are all ultimately helpless to a far greater degree than we dare admit. Our fragility before the forces of nature (both those outside us and those within that cause pain, disease, and aging), as well as the certainty that death is our ultimate earthly destiny, are unbearable to face without some means of consoling ourselves, and of giving meaning and purpose to our lives.

Religion, as well as the sense of belonging to a community, once provided that means for most people. But over the years the progress of science and the development of newer, more efficient modes of production undermined religious faith, as it did the traditional ties between people that, together with religion, made life livable . . . . The older ways did not disappear, but they ceased to exert the exclusive dominance they previously had . . . .

The accumulation of wealth and material comforts, rather than secure rooting in a frame and context, began to form the primary basis for quelling the feelings of vulnerability that inevitably afflict us. Increasing numbers began to base their hopes and dreams on the evident progress in our ability to produce goods . . . .

DECLINE OF FRIENDLINESS

The economist Fred Hirsch noted that a decline in sociability and friendliness has been characteristic of modern economies. He noted that friendliness "is time consuming and thereby liable to be economized because of its extravagant absorption of this increasingly scarce input." Hirsch suggested that the time needed for consumption of all that has become within economic reach may "reduce friendliness and mutual concern in society as a whole" . . . .

'BELONGING' IN COMMUNITY NEEDED

If we are to fashion an alternative capable of luring us away from the attractions (and concomitant costs) of the consumer way of life, clearly restoration of the sense of community and connectedness to others must be at the heart of it . . . . This kind of change will require considerably more attention to context, to support groups, and to the mutual sustaining of values and assumptions . . . .

The consumer society has not left people in higher spirits. Far more than joy or contentment with their present materially comfortable status, Seabrook found disillusionment, sense of hopes betrayed. A sense on the part of parents that they had lost touch with their children; a sense on the part of the children that they had been set adrift; a fear of muggers, rapists, vandals; a diminished sense of being able to count on others for help—these were some of the things that seemed to accompany and to spoil these people's increased affluence. The loss of community is one of the great problems we face as a society, and one of the great burdens for a very large number of individuals . . . .

PEOPLE WHO NEED PEOPLE

Few of us would explicitly avow that we have chosen to rely on products instead of other people, and, fortunately, the bonds of community and interdependency are too important to be severed completely. But the widespread yearning for greater closeness to others suggests that for many there is a sense of superficiality about these connections, even when things look good "from the outside" . . . .

We are faced with having to learn again about interdependency and the need for rootedness after several centuries of having systematically—and proudly—dismantled our roots, ties, and traditions. The tallest trees need the most elaborate roots of all. To make use of our technology in a way that enhances rather than degrades our lives, we must take account of our new understanding of ecological limits and interdependence.

—**Paul L. Wachtel,** *The Poverty of Affluence: A Psychological Portrait of the American Way of Life*. **New Society Publishers, 1989, pp. 60, 61, 62, 63, 64, 65, 66, 69, 166, 167, 169, 170. Used by permission.**)

For Further Reflection

1. Roland Allen, *The Ministry of the Spirit*. Allen (1868-1947) was an Anglican, but the Pauline "in-and-out" ministry approach he advocated challenged the "hunker in" practice of traditional mission efforts. This book is worth its weight in gold.

2. Jay Baer, "Social Media, Pretend Friends and the Lie of False Intimacy," https://www.convinceandconvert.com/social-media-tools/social-media-pretend-friends-and-the-lie-of-false-intimacy/amp/

3. Robert Banks, *Paul's Idea of Community: The Early House Churches in Their Cultural Setting*.

4. Stephanie Bennett, "Choosing Vulnerability," The Secret Place, Nov. 19, 2019, https://www.youtube.com/watch?v=ph3YItmy6sU

5. Ray Allen Billington, *Westward Expansion: A History of the American Frontier* (originally 1929).

6. Peter Block, *Community: The Structure of Belonging*, 2008. Written for the business world, it nevertheless has many valuable insights for believers.

7. Dietrich Bonhoeffer, *Life Together*.

8. Brene Brown, "Vulnerability," https://www.youtube.com/watch?v=iCvmsMzlF7o

9. Ross Chapin, *Pocket Neighborhoods: Creating Small Scale in a Large Scale World*, 2011

10. Jack Deere, "The Pain of Intimacy," cassette, Whitefish, MT, 1996.

11. Thomas Dubay, "Communication in Community," ST, Winter, 1985. ($3.00)

12. S.D. Gaede, *Belonging: Our Need for Community in Church & Family*, 1985.

13. Art Gish, *Living in Christian Community*, 1979.

14. Stanley J. Grenz, *Created for Community*, 1998.

15. Gordon L. Hall, *The Sawdust Trail: The Story of American Evangelism*, 1964.

16. R. Hammett/L. Sofield, "Developing Healthy Christian Community," ST, Autumn, 1996. ($3.00)

17. Bonnie Jaeckle, "The Missing Link: Healing Is Connected to Christ's Life in the Community," ST, 37:1-2, 2011. ($3.00)

18. Hal Miller, *Christian Community: Biblical or Optional?* 1979.

19. Henri Nouwen, "Forms of Hospitality," *Reaching Out: The Three Movements of the Spiritual Life*, 1975.

20. Elizabeth O'Connor, *Call to Commitment: The Story of Church of the Savior*, Washington D.C., 1963.

21. Josef Pieper, *Leisure: The Basis of Culture* (orig. 1952), 2009.

22. Mary Pipher, *In the Shelter of Each Other: Rebuilding Our Families*, 1996.

23. Edward E. Plowman, *The Underground Church: Accounts of Christian Revolutionaries in America*, David C. Cook, 1971.

24. Milt Rodriguez, *The Community Life of God*.

25. Mark Strom, *Reframing Paul: Conversations on Grace & Community*.

26. *The Martyr of the Catacombs: A Tale of Ancient Rome* [Originally, ca. 1876], "Life in the Catacombs," Moody Press, 25th printing, 1982.

27. Elton Trueblood, *The Community of the Committed*, 1961.

28. Jean Vanier, *Community & Growth*.

29. Jean Vanier, *From Brokenness to Community*.

30. Frank Viola, *Finding Organic Church: A Comprehensive Guide to Starting and Sustaining Authentic Christian Communities*.

31. Frank Viola, *God's Favorite Place on Earth*.

32. Jon Zens, editor, The Anabaptists (5 articles), *Baptist Reformation Review*, Autumn, 1978. ($4.00)

33. Jon Zens, *Christ Alone: Five Challenges Every Group Will Face*. ($5.00)

34. Jon Zens, *Jesus Is Family: His Life Together*. ($10.00)

35. Jon Zens, *Life Between the Bookends: Is the Lord's Passion Our Passion Too?* ($5.00)

Jon may be reached at:

jzens@searchingtogether.org

(715) 338–2796

P.O. Box 548
St Croix Falls, WI 54024

Many voices. One message.

Quoir is a boutique publishing company
with a single message: Christ is all.
Our books explore both His
cosmic nature and corporate expression.

For more information, please visit
www.quoir.com

CPSIA information can be obtained
at www.ICGtesting.com
Printed in the USA
BVHW060713300620
582503BV00006B/665

9 781938 480584